Original title:
Infinite Rhythms

Copyright © 2024 Swan Charm
All rights reserved.

Author: Paulina Pähkel
ISBN HARDBACK: 978-9908-1-2647-0
ISBN PAPERBACK: 978-9908-1-2648-7
ISBN EBOOK: 978-9908-1-2649-4

Boundless Beatitudes

In the morning light, hope shines bright,
Whispers of joy take their flight.
The dew-kissed grass, a gentle dance,
Embraces life in a fleeting glance.

Rays of sun, a warm embrace,
Filling hearts with love's grace.
With every laugh, a seed is sown,
In every moment, beauty's grown.

Clouds part ways, the sky unfolds,
Stories of life, eternally told.
In the stillness, peace does dwell,
A sacred place, where all is well.

Mountains tall and valleys low,
Nature's chorus sings its flow.
In the silence, wisdom thrives,
A reminder of how we survive.

Stars ignite with tales untold,
Guiding hearts through nights of gold.
In every heartbeat, light resides,
In boundless beatitudes, love abides.

Loops of Light

In twilight's hush, the colors weave,
Dancing softly, as dreams believe.
Waves of gold in endless flight,
Whisper secrets, loops of light.

Bright beams flicker through the trees,
Painting shadows, a gentle tease.
Moments caught in glowing sight,
Captured softly, loops of light.

Unseen Symphonies

In quiet corners, whispers flow,
Melodies that no one knows.
Harmonies of heartbeats play,
Guiding souls through night and day.

Invisible notes in the air,
Binding dreams with tender care.
Each beat echoes, soft as clay,
Unseen symphonies lead the way.

Threads of Continuous Melody

Woven tightly, a vibrant thread,
Stories told of hearts that bled.
Gentle tunes softly unite,
Threads of melody, pure delight.

With every stitch, a voice takes flight,
Rich with laughter, hope, and light.
In the fabric of day and night,
Threads of melody shine so bright.

Ageless Dance of Frequencies

In the ether, the rhythms sway,
Echoing time in endless play.
Dancing spirits, ancient lore,
Frequencies that we adore.

Every pulse, a timeless call,
Resonating through one and all.
A dance that weaves through every door,
Ageless frequencies, forevermore.

Chasing the Echoing Heart

In the shadows where whispers dwell,
The pulse of dreams starts to swell.
A fading call drifts through the night,
Chasing echoes, seeking light.

Through tangled paths and winding ways,
The heart beats loud in silent bays.
Each thrum a promise, each sigh a spark,
Searching fervently through the dark.

With every step, the rhythm sways,
A melody lost in the haze.
A fleeting glance, a touch divine,
Can we find what's truly mine?

The wind carries tales of the brave,
Of love that flows like a restless wave.
In the chase, we find our worth,
As echoes guide us back to earth.

So we run with hearts open wide,
In this dance, there's nothing to hide.
For in this chase, we find our song,
In the echo, where we belong.

Metronome of the Universe

Stars flicker in a cosmic dance,
Each beat a ripple, a sacred chance.
The universe breathes, a steady flow,
Marking time in the night's soft glow.

Galaxies swirl in a grand parade,
Each pulse a memory lovingly made.
A metronome ticks in endless space,
Counting moments with gentle grace.

What stories lie in the starlit vast?
Whispers of futures, echoes of past.
In the heartbeat of all that's profound,
The music of life can always be found.

Comets trail like fleeting dreams,
In this rhythm, nothing is as it seems.
With each tick, the cosmos sings,
In perfect harmony, the universe clings.

Together we sway in the celestial beat,
As time and space gracefully meet.
In the metronome's unwavering art,
We find the pulse of the universe's heart.

Resonance Beyond the Horizon

Across the hills where skies unfold,
Lies a story yet untold.
A resonance beckons, soft and clear,
Drawing close what we hold dear.

Beyond the edge where shadows play,
A whisper invites us to stay.
The mountains echo, the valleys hum,
In the distance, we hear the drum.

With every breath, we feel the call,
A symphony rising over all.
In the twilight glow, a dance ignites,
As colors blend, the day unites.

Threads of fate weave through the night,
In this harmony, all feels right.
Resonance calls from realms anew,
In its embrace, we find what's true.

So let us chase what lies ahead,
With hearts aligned and dreams widespread.
Together we'll roam in the twilight's font,
As echoes guide our wandering jaunt.

Infinite Cadences

In the rhythm of time, we sway,
Infinite cadences lead the way.
A melody woven into our veins,
Where joy and sorrow share the reins.

Through valleys deep and mountains high,
The notes of existence rise and fly.
Each heartbeat a drum, each breath a tune,
In this concert beneath the moon.

Soft whispers dance in the morning light,
While shadows play in the quiet night.
The song of life, a wondrous thread,
Connected moments, where dreams are fed.

We wade through the sound, hand in hand,
As the world moves to a vibrant strand.
With every step, a new refrain,
In the cadence, we drop the pain.

So let the symphony linger long,
In the inflections, we find our song.
For in the infinite cadence we find,
A harmony that unites all mankind.

The Sound of Existence

In the whisper of the trees,
Life hums a gentle tune.
Stars flicker in the night,
Echoes of a lost rune.

Waves crash upon the shore,
Each a tale to tell.
Time dances with the breeze,
Where shadows softly dwell.

Mountains hold their secrets,
In silence they confide.
Nature sings a chorus,
Of peace within the tide.

Colors paint the sunrise,
A symphony of light.
Every moment a heartbeat,
In the stillness of night.

Life's essence flows around,
A melody so pure.
In every breath we take,
Our souls begin to cure.

Rhapsody in Infinity

In endless space we wander,
Stars weave their cosmic dance.
Galaxies whisper softly,
In the universe's trance.

Comets blaze a bright trail,
Stories etched in the dark.
Each heartbeat's a reminder,
Of the journey we embark.

Time flows like a river,
Upon its hidden crest.
Moments shimmer and fade,
Yet in memory, they're blessed.

Life's a vibrant canvas,
With colors bold and bright.
Every shadow tells of hope,
In the depths of night.

Harmony's sweet resonance,
A symphony divine.
In infinity we find peace,
As stars and souls align.

Footsteps in the Void

In the silence of the night,
Footsteps drift like dreams.
Whispers weave through darkness,
Caught in moonlight's beams.

Stars blink in recognition,
Guiding us along.
Every path we wander,
Becomes a fleeting song.

The void holds ancient secrets,
In shadows they reside.
An echo of existence,
Where thoughts and fears collide.

With each step we discover,
A map that's drawn in light.
The journey's our creation,
As we conquer the night.

In the vastness of the cosmos,
We leave a trail behind.
Footsteps in the void linger,
Etched within the mind.

Timeless Sonatas

In the heart of every moment,
Music softly plays.
Notes drift through the stillness,
Like sunlight's gentle rays.

Every breath a harmony,
A dance of soul and sound.
Life's eternal score unfolds,
In beauty we are found.

Melodies of the seasons,
Each voice a whispered prayer.
Nature sings in rhythms,
In the stillness of the air.

The past and future mingle,
In a waltz of time.
Every heartbeat is a measure,
In the grandest rhyme.

From silence springs creation,
Where echoes intertwine.
Timeless sonatas linger,
In the depths of the divine.

The Unraveling Harmonics

In twilight's soft embrace we find,
A melody that threads the mind.
Each note a whisper from the past,
An echoing truth, a bond to last.

The strings vibrate with tender plea,
Unfolding tales of you and me.
In harmony, our souls unite,
Together we dance, igniting light.

Layers of sound, a gentle weave,
In every silence, hearts believe.
With every strum, the cosmos hums,
As gravity pulls, the rhythm drums.

Dissonance fades as we align,
A symphony where stars entwine.
The universe, a grand design,
In unraveling harmonics, we shine.

Our hearts compose the sweetest art,
Each beat a step, no need to part.
In this symphonic, endless flight,
We find our way through endless night.

Celestial Beats and Heartstrings.

Underneath the silver sky,
Celestial beats begin to fly.
With every pulse, the stars align,
A rhythm where our souls combine.

The universe breathes with each sound,
In cosmic waves, our love is found.
Heartstrings pull, and gently sway,
In the harmony of night and day.

Galaxies twirl to a vibrant tune,
A dance that cradles sun and moon.
As constellations softly sing,
We feel the joy that love can bring.

Through stardust paths, our spirits soar,
Each heartbeat opens every door.
Connected by this vibrant thread,
In celestial beats, our hopes are fed.

So let the music guide our way,
In every note, forever stay.
With every pulse, we rise and fall,
In heartstrings' reach, we have it all.

Eternal Echoes

Whispers of time in silence weave,
Eternal echoes that never leave.
A soul's reflection, like a dream,
Carried forth on memory's stream.

The past is painted in vivid hue,
Each moment breathing, ever true.
From shadows deep, the light will break,
In every echo, choices make.

With gentle hands, we craft and mold,
Through timeless tales, our lives unfold.
In the harmony of voice and sound,
The echoes linger, profound, unbound.

With every heartbeat, truth resounds,
In whispered songs, our love surrounds.
The universe, a canvas wide,
In eternal echoes, we abide.

So let us dance in time's embrace,
Through every pulse, we find our place.
With echoes strong, we'll bravely stand,
As notes interlace, hand in hand.

Melodies Beyond Measure

In every corner of the night,
Melodies rise, a wondrous sight.
Waves of sound that dance and play,
In perfect timing, hearts convey.

Each note a journey to explore,
A symphony that opens doors.
Beyond the time, beyond the speed,
In melodies, our spirits feed.

With chords that bind, we take the flight,
Into the depths of pure delight.
As rhythms pulse within our veins,
In harmony, love's truth remains.

The world may fade, the stars may weep,
But melodies awaken deep.
They swirl around, a sweet embrace,
In every sound, we find our grace.

So let us sing through every dream,
In melodies that brightly gleam.
With every note, we chase the dawn,
In music's heart, we carry on.

Spheres of Eternal Sound

In the stillness of the night,
Whispers weave in soft delight.
Melodies rise, a gentle tide,
Carrying dreams where echoes bide.

Voices dance in twilight's glow,
Harmonies that ebb and flow.
Each note a star, a spark divine,
In this sphere where hearts entwine.

Ripples trace the cosmic sky,
Time dissolves in a sigh.
With every beat, the universe sings,
Crafting worlds on silken wings.

Infinite tones in the air,
Breath of music everywhere.
Eternal sound soars ever free,
In a realm of timeless glee.

Listen close, let shadows blend,
Where the beginning meets the end.
In these spheres, our souls unite,
Bound by sound, we take flight.

Echoes Across the Abyss

In the depths of endless night,
Whispers drift, lost from sight.
Echoes call from a distant shore,
Yearning hearts that seek for more.

Fading sounds of ancient lore,
Reach for stars forevermore.
In the silence, shadows play,
Haunting tunes that drift away.

Beyond the edge of dreams it seems,
Live the hopes and scattered beams.
In the chasm, voices rise,
Reflections of the boundless skies.

Longing souls, they resonate,
In the vastness, chance or fate.
Echoes pulse like distant light,
Guiding wanderers of the night.

Whispers fade in the still abyss,
Yet each tone is a tender kiss.
Across the void, an endless song,
In this silence, we belong.

The Melody of Distant Dreams

In the heart of twilight's grace,
Whispers swirl in a warm embrace.
Distant dreams take flight anew,
Chasing shadows, lost and true.

Softly sung by stars above,
Melodies weave tales of love.
In the silence, echoes glow,
Carried forth by winds that flow.

Drifting clouds on a silver sea,
Cradle hopes and set them free.
Every note a guiding star,
Shining bright, no matter how far.

Visions linger, painted skies,
Within the heart, the music sighs.
Every breath a wish unspun,
In this world where dreams have run.

Awake the spirit, let it soar,
To the rhythm we explore.
In harmonic whispers, we find grace,
The melody of time and space.

Temporal Dance of Light

In the dawn where shadows fade,
Light begins its vibrant parade.
Every hue a story told,
In the warmth as day unfolds.

Moments flicker, softly bend,
Time entwines with every friend.
Through the prism, colors spin,
In this dance, we lose and win.

Chasing rays on summer streams,
Life awakes, igniting dreams.
In the glimmer, joy ignites,
As we twirl through endless nights.

Fleeting moments, softly sigh,
Underneath the vast, blue sky.
Glances shared, and laughter bright,
In the temporal dance of light.

Hold the beauty, let it flow,
For in this light, we come to know.
Time withstands its gentle flight,
As we sway in pure delight.

Unending Melodies

In whispers of the night, we find,
A tune that dances through the mind,
With every note a story spun,
A journey where the heart can run.

The softest winds begin to play,
In colors bright, they gently sway,
Each harmony a fleeting dream,
A river pure, a silver stream.

The echoes call from far away,
In twilight's arms, they come to play,
With every chord that fills the air,
A promise made, a bond we share.

From silent shadows, rhythms rise,
In every heartbeat, love complies,
In memories wrapped, we do reside,
A symphony we cannot hide.

As dawn awakes, the melodies blend,
A timeless song that knows no end,
Through every season, every sigh,
Unending tunes that fill the sky.

Harmonics of the Cosmos

In starlit skies where secrets play,
The universe sings night and day,
Each planet strums a gentle chord,
In cosmic rhythms, we're adored.

Galaxies swirl in endless dance,
Inviting us to take a chance,
In every twirl and bright display,
The cosmos hums, it finds its way.

The moonlight drapes a silken veil,
While comets weave an ancient tale,
With echoes from a distant past,
In harmony, we breathe at last.

In every heartbeat, we align,
With constellations so divine,
In beauty's grasp, we boldly roam,
The harmonics of this vast home.

As night descends and silence reigns,
The music lingers in our veins,
A cosmic score that speaks to all,
In whispered notes, we heed the call.

The Symphony That Never Sleeps

As dawn breaks free from night's embrace,
A symphony begins to trace,
In every moment, every breath,
A melody woven with depth.

The chirping birds and rustling leaves,
Compose a song that gently weaves,
With chirps and sighs—a waking dream,
In harmony, we find the gleam.

The city hums in busy streets,
Each heartbeat where the rhythm meets,
In laughter shared and tears that flow,
The symphony will always grow.

As twilight wraps the world in grace,
The notes transition, set their pace,
With every star, a tune ignites,
In endless nights, our joy ignites.

The timeless dance of night and day,
In every note, we find our way,
A symphony that never fades,
In every heartbeat, love cascades.

Fragments of Perpetual Motion

In morning light, the world awakes,
With every breath, a dream remakes,
The spinning earth, a ball in flight,
In harmony, we seek the light.

The ticking clock, a constant sound,
In every second, life is found,
Each fleeting moment, gold in hand,
A dance of time, anew we stand.

The waves that crash upon the shore,
In rhythmic beats, they ask for more,
With echoes of a timeless flow,
In fragments, life begins to glow.

As seasons shift and colors fade,
In every heartbeat, journeys made,
The past a whisper, future bright,
In fragments, we find pure delight.

In every step, a path unfolds,
In every story, love retold,
Together we move, side by side,
In perpetual motion, we glide.

The Vibration of Endless Corners

In a world where shadows bend,
Curved lines of space transcend.
Every turn a whispered sound,
Echoes of the lost are found.

Colors dance in fading light,
Every edge, a sleepy flight.
Silent paths where dreams awaken,
In those corners, hearts unshaken.

Whispers brush against the air,
Secrets linger everywhere.
Through those folds of time we weave,
Chasing visions, we believe.

Unseen forces gently pull,
In the distance, time is full.
Every angle, every sigh,
Paints the canvas of the sky.

With each heartbeat, walls dissolve,
In this maze, we come to solve.
Endless corners, grace and poise,
In the silence, hear our voice.

Melodic Tides

Waves are crashing on the shore,
Ocean's song forever more.
Rhythms pulse beneath the moon,
Nature's dance, a timeless tune.

Whispers of the rolling sea,
Calling out to you and me.
Melodies of salt and breeze,
Stir our souls with gentle ease.

Footprints fade with every wave,
In their presence, we are brave.
Tides that ebb and flow like time,
Carry dreams in syncopine.

Drifting thoughts as currents sway,
Lost in music, we shall stay.
Waves of harmony align,
In their depths, our spirits shine.

Melodic tides will guide our hearts,
In their rhythm, love imparts.
Together, we will find our way,
In the ocean's endless play.

Timeless Breathe

In the stillness, moments pause,
Breath whispers, without a cause.
Time unwinds, our senses blend,
In each inhale, we transcend.

Hushed reflections in the night,
Stars above, a guiding light.
Every heartbeat, softly felt,
In this space, our fears are melt.

Wisps of dreams like clouds float by,
Each exhale, a gentle sigh.
Holding on to fleeting thoughts,
In this stillness, time is sought.

Life unfurls in subtle ways,
In the quiet, wisdom stays.
Breathe the essence of our fears,
In this moment, find the years.

Timeless breathe, a sacred art,
Inhale deeply, feel the heart.
Connected to the earth and sky,
We find peace as time drifts by.

The Spirals of Harmony

Winding paths that twist and twine,
Nature's breath, a grand design.
In each spiral, echoes gleam,
Life unfolds in every dream.

Harmony in every curve,
Flowing gently, strong and sure.
Round and round the dance of fate,
In the spiral, we relate.

Through the chaos, find the grace,
In each turn, a warm embrace.
Cycles turn and weave through light,
Bringing balance to the night.

Whirling thoughts that twist and sway,
Guiding us along the way.
In the spiral, truth appears,
Cleansing doubts, dissolving fears.

Spirals whisper tales untold,
Holding treasures yet to hold.
In each loop, a life reborn,
In harmony, we are one with dawn.

Circle of Life's Song

In the morning light, we rise,
Awakening dreams beneath the skies.
Nature's chorus softly sings,
Echoing the joy that life brings.

Seasons change, a dance of fate,
Opening hearts, we celebrate.
In every heartbeat, we belong,
United in this vibrant song.

From the womb of earth, we start,
Connected with each beating heart.
Life's tapestry, woven tight,
Guided by the stars at night.

Through laughter, tears, and tender grace,
We find our path in time and space.
Embrace the journey, brave and strong,
Together we sing life's sweet song.

In the twilight's calm embrace,
A gentle peace, a sacred place.
As shadows fade and daylight's gone,
In our hearts, life's echoes throng.

Undulating Whispers

Gentle breezes brush my skin,
Carrying secrets deep within.
Nature's voice, a soft caress,
In its warmth, I find my rest.

The ocean tides, they rise and fall,
Whispers of water, nature's call.
Rhythmic waves, they kiss the shore,
In their song, I long for more.

Leaves that dance upon the trees,
Swaying lightly with the breeze.
Every rustle a story shared,
In each moment, I am bared.

Mountains echo ancient tales,
In quiet strength, the silence pales.
Undulating whispers guide my way,
Through night and light of every day.

In the stillness, I can hear,
Echoes of life, so crystal clear.
Embrace the whispers, let them flow,
In undulating waves, we grow.

Celestial Rhythms

Stars adorn the velvet night,
Celestial rhythms, pure delight.
In the vastness, we roam free,
Dancing 'neath infinity.

The moon's glow, a silver beam,
Guiding dreams by starlit gleam.
Galaxies spin, a cosmic waltz,
In the silence, the universe exalts.

Comets race through the dark abyss,
Every spark a fleeting kiss.
Whispers from the Milky Way,
Remind us of the magic at play.

Planets orbit, time flows on,
In their dance, the sun is drawn.
Each heartbeat syncs with the divine,
In celestial flow, we intertwine.

And as the dawn begins to break,
Shadows flee, and dreams awake.
Celestial rhythms grace our soul,
In the universe, we find our whole.

Threads of Time and Sound

Threads of time weave through our days,
In every heartbeat, in myriad ways.
Moments linger, soft and light,
In the shadows, we find our sight.

Echoes linger, whispers play,
Capturing truths we hide away.
Through laughter shared and silence felt,
In connection, our hearts melt.

Music flows, a river wide,
Notes that carry, like the tide.
In every song, a story sings,
Binding us to what life brings.

As the clock ticks, we move on,
Through the dusk until the dawn.
Threads of sound that wrap around,
In the fabric of love, we are bound.

Embrace the rhythm, let it sound,
In every heartbeat, life is found.
Through dance and song, we come alive,
In threads of time, together we thrive.

The Color of Sound

In whispers soft, hues collide,
The music paints where dreams reside.
Each note a shade, a brush of grace,
Dancing light in every space.

Echoes swirl in bright array,
A symphony that calls to play.
Crimson heartbeats, sapphire sighs,
Violet laughter fills the skies.

Melodies like rivers flow,
Through golden fields, they gently grow.
In rhythm's grip, the colors blend,
A fleeting tune, yet never end.

Shadows pulse with every sound,
In silence, secrets can be found.
With every note, a story spun,
A tapestry of sight and sun.

So let the sound enwrap your soul,
In every hue, you'll find your whole.
A canvas vast, where echoes soar,
The color of sound forevermore.

Strings of Creation

From silence deep, a pluck begins,
The strings vibrate, the magic spins.
Crafted notes through fingers glide,
In every strum, the worlds collide.

A gentle touch brings forth a spark,
With every chord, ignites the dark.
Harmony breathes in pulsing time,
Between the beats, a whispered rhyme.

Threads of gold and silver gleam,
Weaving hopes within the dream.
Each tension pulled, a destiny,
Together twined, in unity.

With every note, the cosmos sways,
In crafted sound, the heart obeys.
Strings of fate, they pull us near,
In melodies, we shed our fear.

In this creation, we transcend,
A resonance that knows no end.
The strings of life, in love's embrace,
We find our place, our sacred space.

Wavelengths of Wonder

Beneath the surface, ripples weave,
Through sound's embrace, we dare believe.
A world unseen, yet deeply felt,
In every pulse, emotions melt.

Vibrations dance in vibrant light,
Unraveling shadows, chasing night.
Each wavelength tells a story clear,
A symphony of hope and fear.

With every echo, horizons shift,
The air alive, a sacred gift.
In the spectrum, colors play,
Illuminating the hidden way.

Wonder flows in every sound,
In whispers soft, we're spellbound.
A fusion of the heart and mind,
In wavelengths, our truth we find.

So let the waves enfold your being,
In endless song, there's no fleeing.
Within the harmony, we'll sway,
In wavelengths of wonder, we'll stay.

Songs from the Beyond

In the whispers of the night,
Beyond the stars, a tune takes flight.
Echoes call, from far away,
Their haunting beauty begs to stay.

Celestial chords entwine the dark,
A melody ignites the spark.
With every note, the cosmos sings,
In timeless dance, the universe clings.

Fragments of light in voices soft,
Reach for the hearts that lift us aloft.
Each song a bridge to realms unknown,
In harmony, we're never alone.

From far-off worlds, they gently weave,
A tapestry of what we believe.
In every harmony, a dream reborn,
Songs from the beyond, eternally worn.

So close your eyes and feel the grace,
In cosmic rhythms, find your place.
Let songs from the beyond cascade,
In the depths of night, our fears allayed.

Echoes from the Abyss

Whispers call from depths untold,
Secrets wrapped in shadows old.
Voices rise like misty breath,
Dancing softly, flirting with death.

Waves of sorrow crash and break,
Memories linger, hearts will ache.
Through the dark, a light draws near,
Echoing softly, drawing near.

Beneath the surface, echoes play,
Woven tales of night and day.
Tales of love, of loss, of might,
Sparkling softly in the night.

In the silence, truths are spun,
Fading softly with the sun.
Echoes fade, but still they cling,
A haunting dance, a ghostly sing.

What lies deep in the blackened sea,
Fragments of what used to be.
In the abyss, light starts to weave,
A tapestry of those who grieve.

Rhythms of the Infinite Sky

Stars will twinkle, rhythms play,
In the night, they drift away.
Clouds dance slowly, dreams take flight,
Whispers echo through the night.

Galaxies spin in silent grace,
Time and space in endless chase.
Celestial bodies twirl and glide,
In this vast, eternal tide.

Cosmic winds weave tales of old,
Stories of the brave and bold.
Comets streak across the dark,
Leaving trails, a blazing mark.

In the dawn, the colors blend,
Heaven's canvas does not end.
With every hue, a new refrain,
Painting echoes in the rain.

Awake, the world begins to hum,
Nature's voice, a perfect drum.
In the rhythms of the sky,
Life's sweet symphony does fly.

Tides of Transcendence

Waves will rise and tides will fall,
Nature's rhythm, magic's call.
On the shore, we stand in awe,
Feeling peace in every flaw.

Salt and sand, they kiss the skin,
Waves of time pull us within.
Moments drift like seashells tossed,
In the currents, love is lost.

Beyond the waves, the horizon waits,
Promises sealed in fate's gates.
In the deep, secrets unfold,
Tales of wonder, ancient, bold.

Sunset's glow wraps all in gold,
Stories heard, yet never told.
With the tides, our spirits rise,
Transcendence found in twilight skies.

As the night brings stars to play,
Embers of dreams that gently sway.
In the dance of night and day,
We find our path, our own way.

The Unraveling Beat

Heartbeats echo, pulse ignites,
Rhythms flow through sleepless nights.
In the chaos, beauty's found,
Life unfolds without a sound.

Threads of fate are woven tight,
Weaving shadows into light.
In the silence, whispers rise,
Unraveling truths in disguise.

Moments flicker, memories stir,
Life's sweet dance, a subtle blur.
With each step, the world spins wide,
In this journey, dreams collide.

As the day gives way to night,
Stars emerge, a dazzling sight.
In the beat of a hopeful heart,
We find our rhythm, play our part.

Through the darkness, light will seep,
Awakening the dreams we keep.
With every pulse, the world's alive,
In the beat of life, we thrive.

The Rhythm of Stars Colliding

In the dark void where silence sweeps,
Stars ignite in their cosmic leaps.
A dance of light, a brilliant show,
As galaxies twist and spin in flow.

Each explosion whispers tales of fate,
Of dreams entwined in an astral state.
In this grand ballet, we find our place,
Among the dust of time and space.

Gravity pulls, a force unseen,
Binding hearts where the light has been.
Orbits chase through an endless night,
Crafting symphonies of pure delight.

The rhythm beats, a cosmic song,
In every heartbeat, we belong.
With each collision, life begins,
As the universe exhales and spins.

A tapestry of chance and choice,
In every star, we hear a voice.
Together in this radiant tide,
In harmony, we shall abide.

Waves of Interwoven Time

Tides that crash on distant shores,
Whisper tales of ancient roars.
In every wave, a story swells,
Of moments lost, of secret spells.

Currents shift, a graceful dance,
Entwined fates in a fleeting glance.
Time weaves strands through every tide,
A tapestry where dreams reside.

Echoes fade, yet still they sing,
Of joys and sorrows that tides bring.
With every ebb, a new chance born,
In the heart of dusk, the edge of dawn.

The ocean holds a timeless sway,
As days drift softly into gray.
Yet in the depths, the pulse persists,
A rhythm found in ocean's mist.

Interwoven through the night,
A dance of shadows, soft and light.
Waves of wonder rise and fall,
In the silence, we hear the call.

Timeless Crescendo

Notes that soar in the evening air,
A melody that banishes care.
In every chord, a heartbeat sings,
A timeless tale that joy brings.

Harmony flows like a gentle stream,
Filling our hearts with its radiant gleam.
As crescendos rise, so do we,
In this symphony of destiny.

Moments blend, a rich embrace,
Time stands still in this sacred space.
Each breath a note, each glance a rhyme,
Together we dance through the sands of time.

Fingers glide on ivory keys,
Awakening echoes on the breeze.
In every twirl, we find our way,
In the song of night, the dawn of day.

With every rise, the spirit soars,
A timeless crescendo that restores.
In every heart, a song to find,
In the music, we are intertwined.

The Pulse of Forever

In stillness lies a beating heart,
A rhythm constant, never apart.
Each pulse a promise, each thrum a dream,
Woven into the endless seam.

Echoes travel through time and space,
Whispers of love, the softest grace.
With every heartbeat, we align,
In the vastness, you are mine.

Timeless moments in a fleeting glance,
Each breath a part of an ageless dance.
As seasons change, our love remains,
A pulse that flows through joy and pains.

The universe hums with life anew,
In every star, a spark of you.
Together through shadows, we shall roam,
In the pulse of forever, we are home.

In each heartbeat, a story told,
A tapestry of dreams we hold.
Through endless nights and bright tomorrows,
Our love transcends all fears and sorrows.

Etched in Time

In shadows deep, our stories weave,
Moments captured, hearts believe.
Memories linger, whispers say,
Time stands still, yet slips away.

Fleeting glances, lost in night,
Faces fade, but love's a light.
Through the years, we hold on tight,
The echoes guide, through dark and bright.

Marks on stone, a tale unfolds,
In every crack, a truth beholds.
Every heartbeat, every sigh,
Tells the tale of you and I.

Worn pages in a book divine,
History written, a sacred line.
Moments shared, through joy and strife,
Each heartbeat, a slice of life.

Chasing dreams, we dare to climb,
All our paths, forever rhyme.
Etched in time, our spirits soar,
In every breath, we seek for more.

Pulsing Eternity

In every pulse, a rhythm found,
The universe, a sacred sound.
Stars align in cosmic dance,
Eternity, a timeless chance.

Waves of light, they twist and twirl,
Space and time begin to swirl.
A heartbeat echoes through the night,
Awakening dreams, igniting light.

Moments captured in a glance,
Infinity sings, inviting chance.
Worlds collide, in passion's glow,
Pulsing life in tidal flow.

Time expands, then contracts tight,
In this cycle, dark and bright.
Threads of fate, we intertwine,
In every breath, eternity shines.

Lost in wonder, we drift and glide,
Holding close, the cosmic tide.
Life's a dance, forever free,
In the heart of eternity.

Carousel of Chords

Round and round, the music plays,
A carousel of vibrant days.
Chords that lift our spirits high,
Melodies that never die.

In the twilight, notes collide,
Whispers soft, like waves, they ride.
Harmony in every beat,
Life's sweet rhythm guides our feet.

Moments shared in perfect tune,
Underneath the shining moon.
Every laugh, a vibrant sound,
In this dance, we all are found.

Voices blend, a tapestry,
Each thread woven, wild and free.
In the air, our hearts ignite,
In the magic of the night.

Feel the rush, let music flow,
Ride the waves, let passion grow.
In this carousel, we soar,
Chords of love forever more.

The Breath of the Universe

Gentle whispers in the night,
The cosmos breathes, a pure delight.
Stars exhale, a cosmic sigh,
In this vastness, we dare to fly.

In every heartbeat, stardust sings,
Creation's pulse, the joy it brings.
Through galaxies, we drift and roam,
Finding in chaos, a place called home.

The wind carries secrets untold,
Mysteries of the young and old.
In every breeze, nature's song,
Guiding us where we belong.

Through the silence, we find our way,
The universe, a bright display.
In every moment, life awakes,
Breath of wonders, for our sake.

Mindful steps through endless space,
In this journey, we find grace.
The breath of the universe, pure art,
Connected deeply, heart to heart.

Undying Waves

Eternal tides crash on the shore,
Their whispers echo, evermore.
In silver foam, the secrets glide,
Carried forth by the ocean's pride.

Beneath the moon's soft, glowing gaze,
They dance and shimmer with gentle ways.
Each crest a tale, each ebb a song,
In their embrace, we all belong.

Time rolls on, yet they remain,
The restless pulse of joy and pain.
A canvas painted by the sea,
Each wave a promise, wild and free.

From stormy squalls to calm retreat,
Their rhythm pulses, strong and sweet.
In every crash, a heartbeat found,
The music of the world renowned.

So listen close, let spirits rise,
In undying waves, the truth lies.
With every break, a story spun,
The ocean's heart beats, never done.

Resonances of the Cosmos

Stars align in an endless dance,
Whispers of time in a cosmic trance.
Galaxies spin, a celestial choir,
Singing of dreams, igniting desire.

Planets waltz in the velvet night,
A symphony paints the dark with light.
Each twinkle speaks of forgotten lore,
Each shadow hints at secrets in store.

Nebulas bloom in colors bright,
Blurring the lines of day and night.
Ether's breath with gentle grace,
Guides us through this vast embrace.

Echoes of worlds that came before,
Everlasting tides on a timeless shore.
The universe sings with vibrant sound,
In its arms, lost hearts are found.

Let your spirit drift and soar,
In the cosmos' arms, forevermore.
In resonances, our souls entwined,
The fabric of fate, beautifully designed.

The Heartbeat of Eternity

Time flows like a river wide,
Carving moments with perfect pride.
In stillness, we feel the pulse,
Of every star, of every impulse.

Whispers linger in the air,
Promises made, intentions rare.
In shadows deep, the echoes play,
A heartbeat marking night and day.

Winds of change softly caress,
In their embrace, we find our rest.
Through every sorrow, every dream,
The heartbeat flows, a gentle stream.

It gathers strength, in laughter's light,
In every corner, dark or bright.
A tapestry of life's embrace,
In its rhythm, we find our place.

So listen close, to love's own tune,
The heartbeat hums, a timeless rune.
In every moment, endlessly,
Eternity breathes, both you and me.

Chasing Shadows of Sound

In whispers low, the echoes play,
Chasing shadows, night and day.
Notes that flicker, then take flight,
In the dim glow of soft moonlight.

Harmonies dance on the breeze,
Carrying dreams like autumn leaves.
Each sound a world waiting to be,
Born from silence, wild and free.

Melodies weave through the air,
Tales of wonder, tales of care.
In every chord, a heart ignites,
Chasing shadows on starry nights.

Rhythms pulse like a distant drum,
Calling forth what's yet to come.
Through every song, we find our way,
Lost in echoes that never sway.

So let us wander, hand in hand,
Through the tapestry of sound so grand.
In chasing shadows, we will find,
The music of the heart, aligned.

Harmonic Eternity

In the whispers of the night,
Melodies intertwine,
Time flows like a river,
Echoes fade, yet shine.

Beneath the moonlit sky,
Dreams waltz in delight,
Stars sing a soft tune,
Illuminating light.

Through shadows, spirits play,
Resonance of the past,
Each note a brushstroke,
Painting moments vast.

Waves crash on the shore,
Ebbing whispers call,
In the tide's embrace,
We rise and we fall.

Together we shall blend,
In harmony's warm grace,
A song that has no end,
In time's sweet embrace.

Solar Flare Serenade

A burst of fiery light,
Dancing across the sky,
With waves that paint the dawn,
As the sun whispers high.

Melodies of the flame,
Igniting hearts anew,
Nature's sweet refrain,
Echoing through the blue.

With every rise of day,
The world begins to sing,
In harmony with time,
As joy takes to wing.

Golden rays cascade,
Bringing warmth to the cold,
Each moment a treasure,
In stories yet untold.

Underneath the sun's gaze,
We dance to love's bright tune,
In the solar flares' pulse,
Our hearts will always swoon.

Pulses in the Algorithm

In the heart of the code,
Patterns twist and weave,
Each pulse a silent beat,
In numbers we believe.

Across the vast expanse,
Data flows like a stream,
Whispers of the machine,
A digital dream.

Connections intertwine,
Bridging gaps unseen,
In binary rhythm,
Life's pulses glean.

With each calculated step,
We dance in the ether,
Crafting our own fate,
As dreamers and creators.

A tapestry of thought,
Knitted by our hand,
In the algorithm's heart,
We forever stand.

Dance of the Timeless Stars

Stars in perfect sync,
Twirl through the velvet night,
Each flicker tells a tale,
Of cosmic love and light.

Galaxies intertwine,
In an eternal waltz,
Nebulae paint the sky,
With colors that exalt.

Gravity pulls us close,
A dance we cannot flee,
Whispers of the cosmos,
In a silent decree.

The universe expands,
In rhythms old and new,
In the heartbeat of time,
We discover what is true.

Together we will twirl,
In the night's embrace,
A dance that knows no bounds,
In this timeless space.

Eternal Echoes

In shadows deep, the whispers weave,
A tapestry of dreams we cleave.
Each breath a note, a soft refrain,
Through time's embrace, we rise again.

Echoes linger, swift and light,
In moonlit hours, through starry night.
With every heartbeat, stories shared,
In silent places, we have dared.

Reflections dance on waters clear,
Memories lost yet ever near.
The past entwined with hopes anew,
In endless loops, we find our view.

Gravity of moments past,
They pull us closer, shadows cast.
With every pulse, a world reborn,
In echoes sweet, we are adorned.

Awake, arise, the journey calls,
Through timeless corridors and walls.
With every echo, find your voice,
In eternal echoes, we rejoice.

Whispers of the Endless Beat

In the stillness, soft and clear,
Whispers of time we hold so dear.
Every tick a moment's grace,
In the rhythm, we find our place.

The heart's cadence, gentle sound,
In its pulse, our hopes are found.
A symphony that knows no end,
In every echo, we transcend.

Beats that resonate through the night,
Guiding souls toward the light.
Every whisper, a guiding star,
Reminding us of who we are.

Through the silence, ties grow strong,
In the beat, we learn the song.
With every breath, we weave the tale,
In the rhythm, we shall prevail.

Endless echoes, a timeless thread,
In each heartbeat, love is fed.
Through whispered dreams, we shall unite,
In the endless beat, pure delight.

The Dance of Timeless Waves

Waves approach with tender grace,
In their rhythm, find our place.
Ebbing tides and rising crest,
In their dance, we feel most blessed.

Whispers of the ocean's breath,
Carry stories beyond death.
Each ripple holds a secret deep,
In their presence, we awake from sleep.

Moonlit paths, where shadows play,
Timeless waves will find their way.
In the crashing, hear the song,
Ancient voices, bold and strong.

Dancing softly, sea and shore,
In their embrace, we ask for more.
With every surge, a lesson learned,
In the tides, our hearts are turned.

Through the waters, life's currents flow,
In the dance, we come to know.
Eternal cycles, rise and fall,
In timeless waves, we hear the call.

Cycles of Celestial Pulse

Stars align in the velvet sky,
In their glow, dreams gently fly.
Each pulse a promise, each turn a fate,
In cycles grand, we participate.

Galaxies spin with silent grace,
In their motion, we find our place.
Celestial hearts beat strong and true,
In this weave, we are born anew.

Among the lights, our spirits soar,
Embracing life forevermore.
With cosmic rhythms guiding hands,
We travel through these endless lands.

In every cycle, stories told,
Of joy and sorrow, young and old.
Across the vastness, echoes fly,
In celestial pulses, we learn to rise.

Here in the stillness, peace we find,
In the heartbeat of the divine.
Cycles weave through night and day,
In celestial dance, we find our way.

Whirlwinds of Rhythm

In shadows of the night, we twirl,
With every beat, our hearts unfurl.
The drums echo deep, a call to dance,
Lost in the music, we take a chance.

Whispers of winds, a soft embrace,
Together we find our sacred place.
Fingers snap, and feet begin to sway,
In whirlwinds of rhythm, we drift away.

The world fades out, just you and I,
Beneath the stars, we touch the sky.
A melody flows, pure and strong,
In this moment, we belong.

The night air hums, electric and bright,
A symphony born from sheer delight.
Unraveled dreams, wild and free,
In dance, we lose our history.

As dawn approaches, we stand still,
With echoes of rhythm, we feel the thrill.
Together forever, hand in hand,
In whirlwinds of rhythm, we make our stand.

The Pulse of the Universe

Stars ignite, a radiant glow,
In silence, all creation flows.
The cosmos hums its ancient tune,
As we trace paths 'neath the silver moon.

Galaxies spin in celestial dance,
Fates intertwine; it's more than chance.
Every heartbeat, a star's refrain,
In the pulse of the universe, love remains.

Time stands still, the past and now,
In the tapestry of fate, we vow.
Whispers of gravity, gently pull,
Through the cosmos, our hearts are full.

Threads of existence, woven tight,
In starlit skies, we find our light.
Every moment, a spark divine,
In this vast expanse, you are mine.

As the galaxies swirl, we take flight,
In the pulse of the universe, all feels right.
Together we soar, across the space,
In the cosmic heartbeat, we find our place.

Dancing in Dissonance

Two souls collide, a spark ignites,
In the chaos, we find our sights.
Notes clash and clash, a haunting sound,
In this dissonance, harmony's found.

Steps unsteady, yet hearts align,
In every misstep, love will shine.
The syncopation of wild beats,
In tangled rhythms, affection meets.

Voices rise high, then crash in despair,
A symphony crafted with daring flair.
Together we laugh, and together we cry,
In dancing dissonance, we learn to fly.

Fears take flight as we break the mold,
In the discord, our love unfolds.
With every stumble, we find our way,
In broken chords, bright colors sway.

As the music swells, we embrace the noise,
In dissonance, we find our joys.
Together we thrive in imperfect grace,
In the dance of chaos, we find our place.

Melodic Legacies

In quiet whispers, stories blend,
Of voices lost and hearts that mend.
Each note a memory, old and new,
In melodic legacies, dreams come true.

The echoes linger, soft like a breeze,
Carrying tales of forgotten trees.
In the fading light, we search for more,
In melodies sung, we find our lore.

Harmonies rise from the ashes of time,
Where every struggle births a rhyme.
With every chord played, we stand tall,
In the legacy of sound, we rise or fall.

Threads of connection, woven tight,
Across generations, love ignites.
The chorus swells, a timeless embrace,
In melodic legacies, we find our grace.

As the final note whispers away,
In our hearts, the music will stay.
Each story told, a gift from the past,
In melodic legacies, our love will last.

Aetherial Echoes

In the sky where whispers fly,
A gentle breeze, a soft goodbye.
Stars twinkle in the quiet night,
Casting dreams in silver light.

Clouds drift by in woven grace,
Time suspends in this vast space.
Memories hum a tender tune,
Echoes dance 'neath the pale moon.

Voices call from realms unknown,
In the aether, seeds are sown.
Each heartbeat sings, a vibrant thread,
Weaving paths where angels tread.

Truth and beauty intertwine,
Through the mist, a sacred sign.
In every note, a story lies,
Infinite beneath the skies.

Light Through Music

Notes alight on fragile air,
Each a spark, a whispered prayer.
Melodies flow like water clear,
Bringing joy, dispelling fear.

Strings vibrate, voices blend,
In each chord, a heart can mend.
Harmony paints the world anew,
Colors bright, with every hue.

Rhythms pulse through time and space,
Life's dance finds its perfect place.
With every beat, the shadows fade,
In the light, our souls are laid.

Lyrics weave a tapestry,
Of love, loss, and memory.
In the silence, echoes play,
Revealing truths in soft ballet.

Endless Dance of the Seasons

Spring unfolds with blooms so bright,
Colors burst, bringing delight.
Summer sun in golden rays,
Laughter shared in endless days.

Autumn leaves, a rustling cheer,
Whispers low as winter nears.
The world transforms in stunning hues,
As nature dons her vibrant shoes.

Winter's chill wraps all in white,
Stars above, a dazzling sight.
In the frost, a stillness grows,
In quiet nights, the heart still knows.

Cycles turn; we dance along,
Seasons hum their timeless song.
Life's movements in perfect beat,
A harmony that's bittersweet.

Vibration of the Soul

Deep within, a pulse does start,
A rhythm flowing from the heart.
Each vibration tells a tale,
Of hope, of love, where dreams prevail.

When silence falls, we hear the sound,
Of every joy that knows no bound.
In stillness, feel the whispers call,
The dance of life connects us all.

Awakened now, the spirit soars,
In the light, the essence pours.
Every breath, a song of grace,
In this vast and sacred space.

Through the layers of the night,
We find truth in inner sight.
Vibrations rise, creating whole,
In the symphony of the soul.

The Loop of Dreams

In whispers soft, the shadows play,
A dance of light, then fade away.
The echo calls from deep inside,
Where hopes and fears in silence bide.

Upon the canvas of the night,
Stars paint our tales in silver light.
Each dream a thread, we weave anew,
In colors bold, in shades of blue.

A spiral path, we journey forth,
Chasing visions of our worth.
With every step, we learn to glide,
In realms where secrets love to hide.

Awake or lost within the quest,
The heart alone knows what is best.
In every loop, a truth revealed,
The depth of dreams, forever sealed.

So let us soar beyond the seams,
Into the vastness of our dreams.
With courage bold, we'll take our flight,
And dance among the stars so bright.

Unbroken Measures

In every heartbeat, time unfolds,
A rhythm deep, a tale retold.
The pulse of life, a steady sound,
In silence wrapped, we are all bound.

Each moment flows, a river wide,
We shape our dreams, with love as guide.
The notes we play, both strong and sweet,
In harmony, our lives repeat.

Through joys and sorrows, we contrive,
In every breath, we feel alive.
The canvas broad, the brush in hand,
We paint our lives, a vivid strand.

Unbroken measures, time unveils,
The strength we find when courage fails.
With every step, we learn to stand,
Together bound, hand in hand.

So let us march, unyielding hearts,
In every end, the new begins.
A melody that never fades,
In unison, our song cascades.

The Heartbeat of Existence

In quiet moments, life persists,
Beneath the noise, the world exists.
Each pulse a flicker, soft and bright,
A testament to endless night.

We breathe the essence of the day,
In simple joys, we find our way.
The dances we share, the tales we weave,
In every heartbeat, we believe.

The gentle touch of love declared,
In fleeting glances, moments shared.
The fabric strong, yet softly spun,
In every life, the threads are one.

To feel the world in rhythmic sway,
In every dusk, in every ray.
A heartbeat echoes through the void,
In every breath, we're not destroyed.

So let us cherish what we're given,
In every heartbeat, we are driven.
Together bound, our lives entwined,
In this existence, love defined.

Threads of Sound in the Void

Between the quiet, whispers sing,
Threads of sound in the dark take wing.
Invisible notes, a melody's grace,
In the vastness, we find our place.

Voices linger in shadowed air,
Echoes of laughter, love, and care.
Each story told, a note profound,
In the silence, there's beauty found.

We dance on the edge of what's unseen,
In shadows' depth, we chase the dream.
With every sound, a spark ignites,
In the quiet, we find our flights.

The threads of sound weave through the night,
In melodies soft, we take our flight.
United in rhythm, hearts all aligned,
In every whisper, the truth we find.

So listen closely, feel the pull,
In threads of sound, the world is whole.
In every echo, we are embraced,
In the void's depth, our hope is laced.

Spirals of Sound

In twilight's grip, the echoes blend,
Whispers of dreams, where shadows bend.
Notes like water, gently flow,
Carving paths through depths below.

Waves of rhythm, embrace the night,
Stars pulse softly, a guiding light.
Melodies dance on the cool breeze,
Inviting hearts to find their ease.

Every note, a life's embrace,
In spiral form, they spin and race.
Around and round, they twist and twine,
Creating worlds where spirits shine.

From silence born, to loud refrain,
In every whisper, joy and pain.
A symphony that never rests,
In constant motion, it invests.

So close your eyes and feel their pull,
Let sounds surround, your soul be full.
For in these spirals, life's profound,
Awakening dreams in spirals of sound.

Celestial Refrains

Up in the sky, the stars align,
With cosmic tunes that intertwine.
A dance of light, a sonorous plea,
Celestial refrains, wild and free.

The planets twirl in rhythmic grace,
Echoing songs from their vast space.
Comets streak with trails of gold,
Carrying secrets of ages told.

In every heartbeat, there's a sound,
A universal pulse, profound.
Softly ringing through the dark,
Igniting souls with every spark.

Galaxies hum their timeless song,
Binding the lost, where they belong.
In the vastness, we all can find,
Celestial refrains that soothe the mind.

So lift your gaze, feel the embrace,
Let the music take you, trace
The constellations, bright and clear,
Finding harmony in the sphere.

The Soundtrack of Forever

Each heartbeat plays a melody,
Threads connecting you and me.
In this life, a score unfolds,
The soundtrack of forever told.

Notes of laughter, soft and bright,
Echo through the silent night.
Memories dance on gentle waves,
A calling deep, each moment saves.

Within the rhythm, time will blend,
Carrying stories, without end.
Each fleeting sigh, a precious gift,
A symphony that makes us lift.

Shores of music, tides that rise,
Songs of love beneath the skies.
When words may fail, our hearts will sing,
A timeless tune, our souls' own wing.

So close your eyes and ride the flow,
Let the sound of forever grow.
For life is music, sweet and rare,
An endless song we all can share.

Unending Melodies

In every dawn, a tune is born,
With gentle light, the day is worn.
A symphony in shades of hue,
Unending melodies, fresh and new.

The rustle of leaves sings soft and low,
While rivers hum in a steady flow.
Nature's chorus, a vibrant spin,
With every breath, the world begins.

From whispered winds to thunder's roar,
Each sound unlocks the ancient door.
In echoes found beneath the skies,
A symphony that never dies.

Through time's embrace, we hear the call,
Unending melodies rise and fall.
They weave together stories bright,
Creating peace within the night.

So let them swirl, embrace the sound,
In every note, pure hope is found.
For life's a song, melodic and free,
An unending dance, you and me.

A Journey Through Timeless Tunes

Whispers of old, drifting in the air,
Melodies pull, with stories to share.
Footsteps echo on the winding road,
Carried by rhythms, lightening the load.

Notes weave a tapestry, rich and profound,
Each chord a moment, where history's found.
Songs of the past float like leaves on a stream,
Inviting us all to dream the same dream.

A dance through the ages, we'll twirl and we'll sway,
The echoes of legends guide us on our way.
In this great symphony, all hearts intertwine,
Bound by the music, our souls in align.

From the quiet whispers to the storms that rage,
The power of music, a timeless sage.
A journey unfolds, each note a new page,
In the book of existence, we all engage.

So let us move freely, together as one,
With every beat, celebrate what's begun.
The journey continues, with timeless tunes,
In the heart of the night, beneath silvered moons.

The Unfolding Song

A melody drifts, touching the soul,
Notes intertwine, making us whole.
Each word, a petal, blooming in time,
This unfolding song, a life in its prime.

Verses emerge, like waves on the shore,
A gentle embrace, we long to explore.
In whispers and echoes, it breathes and it lives,
The magic of music, the love that it gives.

Choruses rise, lifting spirits so high,
As laughter and heartache float up in the sky.
With every refrain, we let go and trust,
For this is our anthem, a journey robust.

So listen with care, let the beauty unfold,
Petals of stories, in colors so bold.
Each note is a treasure, so precious and rare,
In the unfolding song, we find what we share.

Together we sway, under starlit embrace,
With rhythms surrounding, we find our own place.
In every beat echoes, the tale of our song,
The unfolding of life, where we all belong.

Cosmic Cadence

In the vastness above, where stars gently hum,
Galaxies dance, to a beat like a drum.
Time flows like rivers, through dark velvet skies,
As the cosmic cadence makes spirits arise.

Whirling in circles, planets align,
The symphony sings, a celestial design.
Waves of ethereal light shimmer and gleam,
In this cosmic ballet, we're part of the dream.

Each comet a note, in the grand melody,
Painting the heavens with vibrant memory.
As constellations reveal ancient lore,
In the cosmic cadence, we yearn for more.

Drifting through space, we feel the embrace,
Of rhythms unending, all time and all space.
In silence, we listen, as worlds come alive,
In this cosmic dance, we thrive and survive.

With the heartbeat of universes pulsing so bright,
We weave through the cosmos, embracing the light.
In the beauty of movement, our spirits take flight,
To the hum of the stars, we surrender the night.

Fractals of Harmony

In the garden of sound, where echoes entwine,
Fractals of harmony, spiraling in line.
Every note a mirror, reflecting the heart,
In patterns of beauty, we're never apart.

The layers of rhythm, like waves on the sea,
A tapestry woven, uniting you and me.
As melodies blossom, resounding with grace,
In this dance of connection, we all find our place.

Notes spin like petals, around a still core,
Fractals of passion, inviting for more.
With each fleeting sound, a moment to seize,
In the fractals we glide, feeling the breeze.

Chords echo softly, in whispers of light,
Uniting our stories, igniting the night.
In harmony's arms, our fears turn to bliss,
In the fractals of life, we find what we miss.

So let us be one, in this grand interplay,
With every resonance, the music will stay.
In the fractals of harmony, together we sing,
Bound by the magic that music can bring.

Interstellar Echoes

In the dark where silence sleeps,
Stars whisper secrets from the deep.
Galaxies stretch and bend in light,
Echoes of dreams take flight tonight.

Celestial winds carry our sighs,
Painting the canvas of the skies.
In every shimmer, a memory calls,
Interlaced tales where wonder falls.

Cosmic dances, a ballet grand,
Planets twirl at the universe's hand.
A symphony played on strings of time,
Melodies woven, sublime and prime.

Through the void, a gentle stream,
Connects the stars to our shared dream.
Whispers of old in harmony rest,
In interstellar echoes, blessed.

So let us gaze with hearts unchained,
At the tapestry of light that's gained.
Together we sing, we rise, we flow,
In the night, our souls aglow.

The Unfurling Song of Time

Time flows softly like a stream,
Winding through the fabric of dreams.
Each moment a note in the grand refrain,
Playing the song of joy and pain.

Seasons shift in rhythmic grace,
A dance of life in a sacred space.
The petals unfold with each sunrise,
In the garden where love never dies.

Echoes of laughter, whispers of tears,
The melody crafted through all our years.
Each heartbeat a pulse, a lovely chime,
Marking the unfurling song of time.

Stars twinkle gently, counting the days,
Illuminating our winding ways.
In the quiet, a symphony starts,
Tracing the paths of our intertwined hearts.

So listen closely, let your soul soar,
To the timeless cadence we all adore.
For in each moment, a tale is spun,
In the unfurling song, we're all as one.

Tides of Eternal Friendships

As waves ebb and flow on the shore,
So do friendships, growing more.
In tides of laughter, tears, and grace,
We find each other in every place.

The moon whispers secrets to the sea,
In gentle ripples, you and me.
With arms wide open, we embrace the swell,
In this dance of life, all is well.

Hand in hand through thick and thin,
Our bonds unbreakable, strong within.
In the shadows and in the light,
We weather together, find our might.

Carried by currents, we sail afar,
Each shared story, a shining star.
Connected forever, come what may,
In tides of friendship, we choose to stay.

So let the ocean sing its song,
In its depths, we forever belong.
Together we ride, together we glide,
In the tides of eternal friendships, side by side.

Unseen Chords of Existence

In the fabric of life, threads intertwine,
Unseen chords of existence align.
Vibrations hum soft in the night,
Binding our souls in radiant light.

A smile exchanged, a comforting hand,
Echoes of love in a vast, unseen band.
Every heartbeat a rhythm, every sigh,
Connecting us all, as passersby.

In laughter and sorrow, we find our tune,
As shadows dance under the watchful moon.
With every encounter, we learn to see,
The beauty in all, the unity.

Threads of compassion weave through our days,
Creating a song in countless ways.
Though unseen they are, they resonate clear,
In the symphony of life, we hold dear.

So let us cherish these silent chords,
That cradle our hearts with gentle rewards.
For in the unseen, true magic dwells,
In the tapestry of existence, love compels.

Waves of Forgotten Time

In the hush of the sea, whispers roll,
Stories of old, like tides, take their toll.
Echoes of dreams with each gentle wave,
Memories linger, the heart they save.

Footprints washed away in the sand,
Seafarers drift, guided by hand.
The horizon calls out with a sigh,
Beneath the vast, ever-changing sky.

Moonlight dances on the water's crest,
Cradling moments that never rest.
In silence, the currents weave their tale,
Journeying onward, where lovers sail.

Seashells hold secrets in their embrace,
Tales of the ocean, a timeless space.
With each rolling tide, life starts anew,
Waves of the past, both tender and true.

Lullabies of the Cosmos

Stars twinkle softly in the night air,
Cradled in darkness, free from all care.
Galaxies spin in a delicate dance,
Whispering dreams that invite romance.

Planets collide in a cosmic spin,
Harmony born, where all can begin.
Light years apart yet forever near,
In the vast expanse, we conquer our fear.

Nebulae bloom like flowers in flight,
Colors intertwine, painting the night.
A lullaby sung on a silken breeze,
Echoes of love that sweep through the trees.

The moon watches over with silver glow,
Casting its magic where soft shadows flow.
In this grand cosmos, dreams intertwine,
Lullabies cradle us, gentle and fine.

Harmony without Borders

In the heart of the world, a rhythm beats,
Voices unite, where passion meets.
Cultures entwined in a melodic embrace,
Celebrating life in this endless space.

Drums echo loudly, the dancers arise,
Feet on the ground, with souls in the skies.
Languages blend in a chorus of sound,
Harmony flowering, where love is found.

Notes travel far over mountains and seas,
Bridging the gaps with a graceful ease.
Kaleidoscope colors painting the air,
Together we weave a tapestry rare.

Hands clasped tightly, we pulse and we sway,
In the heart of the moment, we dance and play.
Let the music carry us, strong and free,
In harmony's arms, we find unity.

Spheres of Sound

In the echo chamber of night, sounds collide,
Whispers of echoes, a vibrant tide.
Voices converge in a symphonic maze,
Creating a world where rhythm sways.

Notes drift like feathers through the cool air,
Each tone a brushstroke, painting out care.
In spheres of sound, we lose our way,
Finding ourselves in the notes that play.

Melodies linger, like dew on a leaf,
Telling our stories, our joy, our grief.
In the circles of song, our hearts align,
A journey profound, through silence divine.

When the final note falls, stillness remains,
A canvas completed, where love sustains.
In the spheres of sound, our spirits soar,
Together we rise, forevermore.

The Beat Goes On

In the heart of night, the drum beats loud,
Echoing softly, breaking the cloud.
Rhythms of life in a dance unfold,
Stories of dreams and tales untold.

Every heartbeat a pulse, a sign,
Time keeps moving, a sacred line.
Lost in the rhythm of joy and pain,
The beat goes on, like a sweet refrain.

Echoing Through Eternity

Whispers of time in the still of space,
Carried on winds, leaving no trace.
Voices of ancients, a haunting call,
Resonating deeply, touching us all.

Memories flicker like stars so bright,
Each echo a shadow in endless night.
Through the ages, their power persists,
An echoing song that none can resist.

Symphony of the Stars

In the heavens above, the music flows,
A cosmic ballet that nobody knows.
Planets and comets, they dance in tune,
Beneath the watchful gaze of the moon.

Melodies rise from the depths of time,
Chords of creation, a celestial rhyme.
Stars hum softly in the darkened sky,
A symphony sung as the night draws nigh.

Endless Landscape of Sound

Across the hills where echoes collide,
A landscape of sound, an endless ride.
Whispers of wind through the trees at play,
Nature composing in its own way.

Rivers that babble, mountains that roar,
Every corner a voice to explore.
In this vast canvas where silence breaks,
The endless landscape of sound awakes.

Timeless Cadences

In the quiet of twilight's embrace,
Echoes linger in a soft trace.
Notes collide in the gentle air,
Whispers of dreams that we all share.

Moments drift like clouds above,
Carried by the wind's sweet love.
Each heartbeat writes a tale profound,
In this symphony, life is found.

The past and future softly blend,
In rhythms that never end.
With every sigh, with every glance,
We find our place within the dance.

Fleeting shadows, fading light,
Cascading down from day to night.
Yet in these cycles, love remains,
A melody that never wanes.

So let us walk through time's embrace,
Finding joy in every space.
In timeless cadences we hear,
The heartbeat of our hope, so dear.

The Dance of Endless Beats

In the hush before the dawn's first ray,
Rhythms pulse, inviting play.
A million hearts begin to sway,
In the dance that greets the day.

Feet upon the earth's warm floor,
Boundless spirits yearn for more.
Every movement, every spin,
Echoes where the dreams begin.

Breath of life and sounds collide,
Unbroken tides we cannot hide.
The music calls, we can't resist,
In endless beats, we find our bliss.

Stars above, they twinkle bright,
Guiding us through the velvet night.
In the silence, we hear them cheer,
As we dance, we persevere.

So let us sway beneath the moon,
Lost in this glorious tune.
Forever twirling with the sun,
In the dance, we are all one.

Whispers in the Void

In the stillness, secrets sigh,
Ripples dance where shadows lie.
Voids of silence, deep and vast,
Whispers echo from the past.

Stars sit watch, the night expands,
Holding dreams in silvered hands.
Each breath a story, softly told,
In the dark, where time is bold.

Through the whispers, hopes take flight,
Shimmering like the morning light.
Fragments linger, lost in time,
Notes of love in softest rhyme.

Every heartbeat thus confides,
Wonders hidden, where love resides.
In the quiet, we depart,
And find solace in the heart.

So listen close, and you will find,
A universe so intertwined.
In whispers, we shall always roam,
For in the void, we find our home.

Cycles of Celestial Song

The sun awakes, the sky ignites,
In swirling hues of dawn's delight.
Celestial bodies drift and glide,
In harmony, they turn the tide.

Each hour brings a brand new tune,
A symphony beneath the moon.
Stars align in perfect grace,
We dance within their vast embrace.

Galaxies spin in cosmic waltz,
A rhythm that never halts.
In every heartbeat, every breath,
A cycle whispers life and death.

Through the ages, echoes ring,
Life's refrain in everything.
In shadows cast and light bestowed,
We learn the steps; we share the road.

So let this song forever play,
Guiding us on our way.
In cycles vast, both dark and bright,
We find our peace within the night.

The Whispering Universe

In starlit skies, secrets unfold,
Galaxies dance, stories retold.
Cosmic winds, they gently sigh,
Whispers of time, forever nigh.

Nebulas bloom, colors bright,
Dreams travel through endless night.
Each twinkle bright, a promise made,
In the universe, love won't fade.

Planets spin in silent grace,
In the vastness, we find our place.
Shooting stars, fleeting and rare,
Carrying wishes through the air.

Eternal echoes drift and play,
Guiding lost souls on their way.
In shadows, light starts to gleam,
Awake, we flow in the dream.

The universe hums a tender tune,
Beneath the watchful, silver moon.
In cosmic arms, we are embraced,
In the whisper, we find our space.

The Infinite Waltz

In twilight's glow, we start to sway,
Steps of the heart, lost in play.
Infinite rhythms guide our feet,
Two souls entwined, a dance so sweet.

The stars align in perfect time,
Twirling together, the air's sublime.
With every spin, our spirits rise,
In this waltz, we're free, no ties.

Each heartbeat echoes in the night,
A timeless dance, pure delight.
We glide through dreams, the world fades,
In this embrace, love never evades.

As moonlight bathes the silent ground,
Soft whispers of promise abound.
With every twirl, the universe smiles,
In the infinite, we walk for miles.

In every step, a story we weave,
Understanding only souls conceive.
Together we flow, forever entranced,
In the infinite waltz, we are danced.

Harmonic Spirals

Spiraling thoughts, like winds that blow,
In patterns of life, we ebb and flow.
Each curve a lesson, sweet and bright,
In harmonic whispers, guiding light.

The universe spins, a delicate spree,
Revealing the truth of you and me.
In spirals of time, we find our way,
Through shadows of night, into the day.

Chords of existence, a melodic race,
Entwined together in space we trace.
Every twist crafted, every turn made,
Resonating waves, love won't fade.

Within these spirals, we rise and fall,
Echoing wisdom, a universal call.
In the dance of atoms, we belong,
Harmonic patterns, forever strong.

So let us spiral, hand in hand,
Through the universe, across the land.
In each revolution, a tale to spin,
With harmonic rhythms, we begin.

Pulse of the Timeless Night

In the stillness, night reveals,
A pulse so strong, the heart it steals.
Stars awaken, softly ignite,
Guiding the dreamers of the night.

Moonlight dances on the lake,
Whispers of secrets, it would take.
Every shadow holds a sigh,
Echoing softly, a lullaby.

Time slips away, like grains of sand,
In the timeless dark, we hold hands.
Immortal moments, forever near,
In the stillness, we lose our fear.

The universe hums, a soothing sound,
In the night's embrace, love is found.
Each heartbeat synced to the cosmic bruise,
In the pulse of night, we choose.

So let us linger, let time stand still,
In the quiet hours, we find the thrill.
Through the endless darkness, we will soar,
As the pulse of the night opens its door.

Boundless Harmonies

In fields where wildflowers sway,
The breeze hums a gentle tune.
Stars whisper secrets at night,
Life dances beneath the moon.

Voices blend in sweet refrain,
Nature's song, an endless call.
Heartbeats echo through the wood,
Reminding us we are all.

Lifted high on wings of dreams,
Together, we rise and fall.
Harmony in every breath,
A symphony for us all.

Through valleys deep and mountains grand,
The music carries afar.
In every heart, a rhythm beats,
An unbroken, shining star.

Boundless is the joy we share,
In unity, we find our way.
Life, a canvas rich with hues,
In boundless harmonies, we play.

Unbroken Waves of Sound

Across the shore, the tides arise,
In echoes of the ocean's cry.
Waves crash with beautifully wild grace,
A timeless lullaby up high.

Each swell carries tales of old,
Whispers of adventures grand.
The sea sings of journeys bold,
Binding us to this vast land.

With every pulse, the rhythms grow,
The heartbeats blend with nature's flow.
Unbroken waves of pure delight,
In the melody, we glow.

From shore to shore, the music spreads,
A call to those who seek and roam.
In salty air, we find our peace,
The ocean's sound, our sacred home.

Together in this vast embrace,
We lose ourselves in ocean's dream.
In unbroken waves, we find truth,
Life's beauty flows like a stream.

Ancestral Chants

In shadows of the ancient trees,
Echoes of our past resound.
With every whisper of the leaves,
Ancestral chants can be found.

Through fires burning, stories rise,
Carried on the winds of night.
In every heart, a tale resides,
A legacy, a guiding light.

Songs of struggle, love, and loss,
In melodies, we find our roots.
Ancestral threads weave through our days,
Uniting branches, ancient shoots.

From generations, voices soar,
In harmony, we gather near.
With every note, we honor those,
Whose wisdom lingers, ever clear.

These chants remind us of our place,
In history's vast, flowing stream.
With every chord, we find our strength,
In ancestral chants, we dream.

The Pulse of Existence

In silence deep, the world awakes,
Each heartbeat marks the time we share.
The pulse of life in every breath,
Connecting us, a bond so rare.

From dawn to dusk, the rhythm flows,
In colors bright, the day unfolds.
Each moment counts, each second sings,
A story woven, yet untold.

The earth beneath, the sky above,
In harmony, they weave and spin.
The pulse of existence beats loud,
A canvas rich, where dreams begin.

Through laughter shared and tears set free,
The pulse unites both near and far.
Together, we dance through this life,
In every step, we find our star.

So listen close, to your own heart,
In every rhythm, find your song.
The pulse of existence calls us forth,
In love and joy, we all belong.

Cosmic Waves of Sound

In the silence, ripples awake,
Echoes travel through the dark lake.
Stars whisper tales of the night,
Soft vibrations take their flight.

Galaxies hum a gentle tune,
While comets waltz under the moon.
Each tone weaves a story new,
In cosmic dreams, our spirits flew.

Lightyears away, their voices blend,
As stellar winds, their notes extend.
Melodies of the vast unknown,
In waves of sound, the truth is sown.

Every breath of space holds joy,
Unraveled mysteries, they'll deploy.
A symphony, both fierce and grand,
The universe writes with its hand.

From black holes to the radiant sun,
In every heart, the pulse has begun.
Let the music guide our way,
In cosmic waves, we learn to play.

The Dance at the Edge of Infinity

Over horizons where time stands still,
The dancers gather with fervent will.
Each step a spark, each twirl a chance,
Together they weave a timeless dance.

Under starlit skies that stretch far,
Their movements shine like the brightest star.
In every turn, the world dissolves,
As mysteries of the cosmos revolve.

A rhythm pulses with every breath,
In twilight's glow, they flirt with death.
Yet in this space, there is only light,
A cosmic ballet that feels so right.

With every leap, a story unfolds,
Of galaxies born and legends bold.
They whisper secrets of what's unseen,
In the moments between, they glean.

As dawn breaks softly, they intertwine,
A fleeting glimpse of the divine.
At the edge of all that is known,
They dance the truth, forever shown.

Whirls of Unseen Frequencies

In the air, whispers hum and glide,
Invisible waves, a cosmic tide.
They swirl around, a secret sound,
Connecting hearts where love is found.

Colorful spirals of pure delight,
Brushing our souls in the quiet night.
Each pulse a promise, soft and clear,
Drawing us close, we feel no fear.

From the depths of silence, they arise,
Awakening dreams beneath the skies.
A dance of colors, a burst of light,
Unseen frequencies take flight.

Echoing through the fabric of time,
In every shimmer, a story to rhyme.
The universe sings; can you hear?
In every note, we hold each dear.

Let us embrace this vibrant sound,
Whirls of energy that abound.
For in these depths of the unseen,
We find the truth where we have been.

Rhythm of the Unwritten

In every heartbeat, a tale unfolds,
A rhythm untold, a dance of old.
With whispered secrets carried away,
In the silence, the words will stay.

Pages unwritten, yet dreams will scream,
As wild as the wind, as soft as a dream.
Let the verses form as they will,
In thought's embrace, we find our thrill.

Each moment captured, a fleeting spark,
Light against shadows, a brush in the dark.
From ink to paper, the flow is free,
Every word breathes, every line sees.

Unseen stories in the air we share,
Crafting the future with utmost care.
In the rhythm of truth, we unite,
Together we write, igniting the night.

So let the music guide each pen,
With every stroke, our spirits blend.
In the harmony of what's been sought,
The rhythm of life, a dance of thought.